I0486531

DATESTAMP:

28 March 2022 Thoughts to Word or Audio. Volume III

The breakthrough of the century. How to decode brain thoughts step by step. The definite guide. Processes and procedures.

Signed David Gomadza

First Global President of the World.

First Datestamp 28 March 2022

Second Datestamp 12 April 2022

Third Datestamp 10 March 2023

ISBN-13: 978-1-4477-9760-9

This is Volume III and must be read in conjunction with the following books.

Volume I.

Thoughts to Word or Audio. How to know exactly what someone is thinking.

ISBN-13: 979-8703923498

Volume II.

Decoding Thoughts and Inner Voice: Explanations

and Debunking the Misconceptions.

ISBN-13: 979-8801455488

In regard to the patent this is the detailed explanation of the patent in Volume I: Thoughts to Word or Audio. How to know exactly what someone is thinking.

ISBN-13: 979-8703923498 dated 28 March 2022

This method was tried and evaluated and works miracles. The only definite and only way to decode thoughts word by word.

DEDICATION

A better future for all.

ACKNOWLEDGMENTS

To Tomorrow's World Order

DATESTAMP:

28 March 2022 Thoughts to Word or Audio. Volume III

Ladies and gentlemen, I can say with much confidence that we have finally tested our method in the first book with a Datestamp / Timestamp of 28 March 2022 titled *Thoughts to Word or Audio. How to Know Exactly What Someone Is Thinking.* I can say for sure that we have finally decoded the language of the brain when thinking and dreaming and from today [15 March 2023] we know everyone's thoughts.

No joke.

Today humanity is able to communicate simply because over centuries humanity has devised a language pattern that is understood by all and is able to be reproduced and understood so that communication between people is easily understood.

Likewise, we can devise a method that the brain uses so that we will be able to talk and understand this language even without spoken words. The brain yes has its own language of which we did not understand until now.

Yes, the brain has its own language that it uses to talk and communicate in order to carry out so many functions and activities.

The human language uses vocals, etc. An alphabetical order. A language construction pattern and rules. Likewise we are going to do the same and come up with a language pattern which we will make universal so that the whole world will know and understand so that when we communicate through brain thoughts then we will all be able to understand each other. Myself as the First Global President of the world this is my first duty. To go deeper than any man has ever been and after that take you all to the next stage of development. A stage so advanced that all I need to do is look at you and know exactly what you are thinking.

This is possible now as of the Datestamp 28 March 2022.

First, I will propose a working hypothesis to work with so that it will make sense at the end. No matter what. No matter who you are or what language you speak, the brain has one language. Just like the vocal language we speak the brain uses sound as well but not in the form we know it.

I argued in Thoughts to Word or Audio that the body has three systems.

1. The system we know with ears, mouth, brain etc.
2. An internal system that works opposite the main system. This system is like our image in the mirror. What we feel on the right side of the body. This inner system feels the same but on the left side of the body. It is like this inner system is looking at us.
3. The third system is what I call the invisible system. The one that is everywhere and can be our main system the one mentioned above. Or the inner system [two] above. This system is the answer in decoding thoughts and even dreams. This system uses both the main and the inner systems, but its system has different properties.

When we speak, what we say is in the form of a sound wave. In the inner system this is converted to light waves. But in the magic part of the body, one that will tell us the secret language of the brain, this becomes electromagnetic waves that are converted to light waves or acoustic waves.

This is the secret.

Once we know that all three systems hear the same message we speak as sound waves but in their own format that means we can find the corresponding message as area specific to know what is going on.

When we think even without saying words. A message is emitted by the brain that corresponds to exactly what we are thinking but this is in the language of the secret system.

The biggest breakthrough is that this emitted sound can be recorded, measured, and decoding to know exactly what a person was thinking at the very moment it was recorded word to word.

This is the opening of the pandora box. A secret revelation that will change the world as I write this.

I promised in Tomorrow's World Order [2019] and in the Greatshift that 2023 is a great year where we are to achieve a lot of world's first. The first global president [myself of course]. A breakthrough in using thoughts as an operating system to drive and operate devices, vehicles etc. A year where we will shift to sustainable energies. A big shift to electrical vehicles etc. A year where we will solve the Russia Ukraine problems to pave the way for peace forever. A year full of great things. Where humanity will understand that we can do better as a people. A year where we will start the journey to the next stage of development.

Tomorrow's World Order

https://play.google.com/store/books/details/David_Gomadza_Tom orrow_s_World_Order?id=VDauDwAAQBAJ&gl=GB

The Greatshift

https://play.google.com/store/books/details/David_Gomadza_THE_GREATSHIFT?id=KH2xEAAAQBAJ&gl=GB

Time is precious so I will get down to the details.

First, we must construct a language pattern which the brain uses. A pattern we can easily understand. A language we can easily interpret. A language that is so natural to humans like speaking that sometimes we do it without even thinking about it. Ever been in a situation where you speak aloud even in your sleep that is unconsciously. This is the equivalent language we want to train our brain to understand so that sometimes it does speak to us even in its sleep as well but a language we can understand.

The great news is that the brain controls everything but most of this relevant to us and similar to speaking is the use of body parts and motion. A person or animal can easily move body parts, legs, jaws, and eyelids etc. even in sleep. So, our language must incorporate motions of body parts as basic.

But the body has over eighty-six billion neurons that speak to different parts of the body. At first that makes everything look impossible. How can we measure and know which neurons are firing and communicating with the body parts?

This is what all the researchers are trying to do hence why up to now no one has produced a solution but us. Most methods I came across measure the area of the brain to decode thoughts.

Pay attention all that is flawed. A brain is capable of firing a billion neurons a time and a brain can think several things per a fraction of a second and so these methods are flawed. So how do we solve this problem?

Guess what? I have already explained what to do in the first book, Thoughts to Word or Audio.

We must use technology readily available to us and manipulate it in order to know exactly what a person is thinking at a given point in time. Refer to this book.

https://play.google.com/store/books/details/David_Gomadza_Thoughts_To_Word_Or_Audio?id=q2xmEAAAQBAJ&gl=GB

But the great breakthrough is that everything the brain does it gives it a specific name and location in the brain. The brain arranges every single word, name, verb etc. in a specific way that it is characterized by a specific sound and above all a specific place in the brain. This is fantastic as you will find out in that this becomes the only exact way also of helping us decode thoughts with such precision that we will know exactly what a person was thinking at a specific point in time and place.

1. The brain arranges all words and everything used in communication in order and specific for that word, function etc. and gives an exact location in the brain. That means every word has a specific place in the brain where the brain just jumps there to locate the word etc. This is critical in decoding the brain. Once we have known that every word etc. used in communication has a specific place in the brain, we then use this point reference as a basic construction of the language of the brain.

2. A brain can multitask and think about a thousand thoughts per minute. The current methods lack this attribute hence

the difficulties of knowing exactly what a person was thinking. All current decoding methods suggest electrodes put on top of the brain to know what that person is thinking? Do you know some critical thoughts are generated deep inside the brain? So, measuring the surface of the brain is flawed outright. Time is therefore critical. By incorporating a time element to argument the space element above enables us to say for sure that we can know exactly what one was thinking at a given point in time.

3. The language of the brain involves some form of motion. Since the brain is a living matter it interprets emotions and this is part of its language. So our language will involve the place element; the part of the brain where the element is stored. A time element. When exactly did the person think about this thought? Therefore, the third element involves some kind of movement.

4. Or fourthly the aftereffects of the motion as part of the language. Since the body is matter such as the brain, whatever movement or emotions has a resultant effect that we can use to know where the brain has gone to retrieve thoughts and what the motion pattern is like to be able to understand the motion of the brain. The idea being that if the brain moves to the front of the brain to locate the word a person was thinking about. A direct result of that movement produces an effect usually in the opposite direction in the form of vibrations. So, vibrations are an end result of a motion. So, if the brain moves to locate the area a person is thinking about. There will be vibrations of some kind as the matter moves.

5. This is critical but something you will love as you start to understand our method. This is because the brain communicates to the rest of the body through neurons that send messages to intended recipients, the parts of the body. This makes constructing brain language easy. The trick is to

know that every time a brain thinks about a thing, an activity etc. It generates two messages. One to locate the area of that function in the brain. The other to locate the body part or area of the body. If you think about sex the easiest thing for all. The brain locates the place in the brain where the word sex is specifically located. At the same time neurons activates the part of the body where sex functions are. So the area of the brain is alighted as well as the sex organs. Another critical point is that when the brain thinks about something e.g., sex. It also sends commands towards the sex organs even if the commands are not acted upon.

So, to construct our language. The language must have the following;

1. A place exactly in the brain where the thought is located.
2. A vibration effect is usually heard in the right ear as a result of that motion if word is located in the right side part of the brain and opposite.
3. The organs or place of the body the brain is thinking about or the organs or parts that will perform that function or help to see that the function is achieved.
4. The commands the brain will give are in the form of emotions.
5. If acted upon the resultant effect of thinking about that and the result of the commands. A man thinking about sex will have the place where sex is stored in the brain lit on the fMRI scans as well as areas where the vibrations are absorbed, usually ears. The sexual organs and the effect of increased blood flow to the organs and the resulting erection etc.

Likewise we are going to include most of the above as part of the communication language of the brain.

To understand any language we define what a language is. We give it rules and construction properties etc. so that we can determine the language and understand it. This can enable us to even predict what a person is going to say after saying the first words in a language. E.g., if a woman bought clothes for herself we can tell or predict how she is going to say that to us. This is because we know the language construction and pattern. We can predict that she is going to say that she bought herself a dress. We do not expect her to use language patterns associated with men etc. or to refer to herself as he. Likewise, the brain arranges words and languages according to sex.

The right side is used to store everything to do with the name man. He is stored on the right side. Likewise, everything to do with a different sex is stored in the left side of the brain. But common things can be stored either side depending on what it is used for and other associations.

There are words, etc. that you can find in various parts of the brain. I will elaborate later.

The brain divides the brain into four huge segments. The front left side, the front right side. The back right side and the back left side. Some words are stored in every one of the four segments, but these are used specific with what that segment is commonly used for.

So, to sum up what you have learnt so far. The brain is a complex structure but one that arranges words in an easily recognized system and classification. This enables us to easily develop a language of the brain that involves up to five key points. Place, resulting effect of movement as in motion such as vibrations, the area of the body concerned with that thought. The given commands to that organ. Whether the command is acted upon and the resultant outcome. To some extend also the resultant emotion in terms of vibrations.

Let us look at an example that has become common nowadays that of using clapping of hands to turn on or off switches to switch light on. This is a good workable solution, one which we can easily use through substituting the clapping of hands with the thinking of clapping of hands as a switch to switch on lights.

Clapping of hands involves a specific word. Clapping which the brain will store in the brain in the right back segment of the brain. This is the area where it stored most words used on a daily basis etc. I will deal with this in detail later.

So, our language will have a back right segment as part of the language construction.

Secondly, clapping effect produces vibrations that the ear can hear first even before it acts upon the noises made by clapping. But I said that the brain will store the word clapping on the right back segment of the brain. So only the right ear vibrations will be loud enough to our language construction pattern to be a matter to us.

Thirdly we must incorporate the commands to be given that will make the hands clap. We must include the parts of the body that does the clapping. The hands do the clapping.

We need a motion. To make the sound. The hands must come together. This is the only way a clapping sound is released.

Fourthly we need to incorporate the result of clapping and we might include a direction of the motion.

Lastly what happens to the sound that is released as claps. So, we need a resultant effect. The sound is absorbed by the body. Do you know I explained in Volume I that sound waves we speak in the body are converted to electromagnetic waves to be interpreted by the inner system and as light or acoustic waves to be able to be interpreted by the third secret system. But the tricky part to understand is that the body does not change electromagnetic waves but instead simply absorbs these waves and then reemits these. So, the absorption process produces vibrations which we can feel if amplified so this becomes part of the language of clapping.

In general, language explains what happens to say; for example, what happens when we clap. One can say that the brain locates a place in the right back side of the brain that sends messages to the hands. But before the message reaches the hands first the right ear vibrates to the clapping as a stored effect even before the actual clapping. This is because this is an already stored function. The brain to be able to store clapping in the right side of the brain must include what clapping is. So, clapping produces vibrations in the right ear. This is a way the brain uses to make sure that each function is stored correctly. Picture a sort code of an account in the banking system. So even if the person is just thinking about clapping. To identify the exact place in the brain where clapping is stored the brain assigns vibrations of clapping as a check-sum function for accuracy purposes.

So, the next stage of language construction is vibrations in the right ear.

Third part is the commands given to do the clapping. These are manifested in the elbows. Both the right and left. Usually sequencing starts with the right side for this specific command.

So, the next language part is the entry point in the elbows.

The fourth language part is the emotion. That is the bringing of the hands together. This produces the clapping. So, hands together.

The fifth part is the sound generated by the clapping and its direction of movement. The clap sound goes down to the ground to be absorbed. So, a downward emotion can represent the direction of the clap.

Sixth we need to include the vibrations generated as the sound of clapping is absorbed. So, vibrations can complete our language construction.

So, this command can represent clapping in the brain.

Once all these sequences are played from first to the last vibrations the brain can easily decoding this as clapping and point to the exact place of the brain where it stores the word clapping.

This is how the brain works.

But the brain has eighty-six billion neurons with billions acting at one time. The brain therefore uses sequencing to distinguish different activities. If the sequence matches what it has stored as clapping, then that is clapping to the brain.

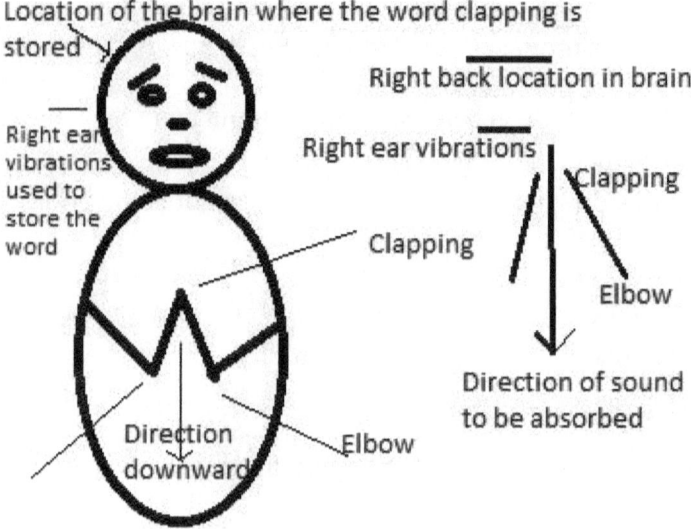

I explain in detail in the first Volume that even if we think the brain emits waves, but these are not as sound. These are electromagnetic waves that are converted to light and acoustic sound. The remarkable thing about all this is that these waves can be recorded and decoded to hear exactly what the person's brain emits at that very moment the person thinks about clapping.

This is the sound emitted when one is thinking about clapping. This in our language we have constructed above. One that is called clapping. So, if you play this sound the brain will itself construct the diagram above.

So it will locate the place in the brain to the right back where it stores the word clapping. Once it has identified this place in the brain. It acknowledges that the place is correct by making vibrations in the right ear. Mind you as a storing classification verification system. We ask the brain to give us something that is referred to as a check code. That proves that the location is the exact location. A requirement of the classification systems. So, the brain, to acknowledge that this is the correct system, will say I want to access clapping in the right back side of the brain. The system says what is the check code. The brain then says vibrations in the right ear. The system listens to the vibrations and says yes. Correct checksum code. Access granted.

Once inside, the brain sends commands to the elbow to activate the hands so that the hands clap.

So both elbows are part of the language of clapping. So, the brain points by pressing the elbows starting with the right-hand elbow. The brain now points to the clapping as the act that will produce the clapping sound. So the system will show you hands together.

The resultant sound noise is directed downward to be absorbed by the ground. So, the body performs the downward motion.

But once sound is absorbed it vibrates on impact. So the system must perform the mild vibrations to indicate that the sound of clapping will be absorbed by the ground. This is because there are somethings where the sound effect generated is not lost. As such that changes the meaning of the word.

So, to be able to do all this we must find a way to include mild vibrations in our language system.

We need to provide the feeling of motion as a directional element.

The spoken language is characterized by alphabetical order and words that describe emotions etc.

Our language will have different effects of activities e.g., feelings and effects of vibrations. Movement of motion stuff etc.

First, we must create stencils of what clapping is.

We need to record sound waves when we say clapping. A voice recorder can be the best instrument to use. We must find a way to incorporate what happens when one claps.

In the first book I discussed how we can use an invented gadget described in this book with recording properties to record what the brain feels when one thinks of clapping and actually claps. Now just thinking about this process of clapping will recall the stored effect of clapping. So, the brain knows what sequence is followed.

I explained in detail in this book that we must have a time element to be able to know what a person is thinking at a specific point in time. I argued that all current methods lack this foresight hence the reason no one has come up with a working method but us. I explained about the delayed time-space continuum mechanism. This stipulates that a point in time and space can be revisited to determine what happened at that point of time and place. This takes advantage of the fact that there is a few second gap between events taking place and before the event is emitted back to earth by the satellite system.

This fact as well makes it possible to superimpose what has already happened with what is happening now so that the two events appear as if occurring at the same time.

I can record a woman in the shower rubbing herself. Then wait for a house mate to use the same shower then superimpose the woman's sounds when she was rubbing herself while taking a shower with the actual man's sounds when taking a shower so that the two appear to be happening at the same time and place in time. Even though the woman had already left the shower cubicle.

This will enable us to create stencils where we can say for sure what one was thinking at the time. We can superimpose the MRI recordings on two occasions but thinking about the same thing. We can ask subjects to think for a specific minute about, say, driving a car. After some time then ask the man to think only about driving a car. Then compare the two MRI recordings and compare these. So that our stencil will point to exact activity to be able to decode this.

I explained that in the first book that the device I invented makes it possible to not even worry about inserting electrodes in the head or brain itself. The device I invented uses electromagnetic waves. In other words, this acts as the miniature fMRI. One that can measure brain activity. But the position must be perpendicular to the head. The device is placed in the lumbar bone where there are less risks of nerve damage only in relation to the other option of operating in the brain.

We can read the brain activity and know exactly what a person is thinking using a device located in the lumbar bone manipulating what we know about physics.

*Classically, electromagnetic radiation consists of **electromagnetic waves**, which are*
synchronized oscillations of electric and magnetic fields.
Depending on the frequency of oscillation, different wavelengths of the electromagnetic spectrum are produced. In a vacuum, electromagnetic waves travel at the speed of light, commonly denoted c. In homogeneous, isotropic media, the oscillations of the two fields are perpendicular to each other and perpendicular to the direction of energy and wave propagation, forming a transverse wave.

Wikipedia.

Maxwell's equations[edit]
James Clerk Maxwell derived a wave form of the electric and

magnetic equations, _thus uncovering the wave-like nature of_ _electric_ _and_ _magnetic fields_ _and their_ _symmetry_. _Because the speed of EM waves predicted by the wave equation coincided with the measured_ _speed of light_, _Maxwell concluded that light itself is an EM wave._[9][10] _Maxwell's equations were confirmed by_ _Heinrich Hertz_ _through experiments with radio waves._

He realized that light is a combination of electricity and magnetism and thus that the two must be tied together. According to _Maxwell's equations_, _a spatially varying_ _electric field_ _is always associated with a_ _magnetic field_ _that changes over time._[12] _Likewise, a spatially varying magnetic field is associated with specific changes over time in the electric field. In an electromagnetic wave, the changes in the electric field are always accompanied by a wave in the magnetic field in one direction, and vice versa. This relationship between the two occurs without either type of field causing the other; rather, they occur together in the same way that time and space changes occur together and are interlinked in_ _special relativity_. _In fact, magnetic fields can be viewed as electric fields in another frame of reference, and electric fields can be viewed as magnetic fields in another frame of reference, but they have equal significance as physics is the same in all frames of reference, so the close relationship between space and time changes here is more than an analogy. Together, these fields form a propagating electromagnetic wave, which moves out into space and need never again interact with the source. The distant EM field formed in this way by the acceleration of a charge carries energy with it that "radiates" away through space, hence the term._

Wikipedia.

Further reading. Click.

_https://en.wikipedia.org/wiki/Electromagnetic_radiation_

I explained in my book that what no one has discovered until now is the fact that when we speak the brain converts sound waves to electromagnetic waves as well as light waves but in the form of acoustic waves in the brain when we think. Since electromagnetic waves travel and occupy the same space as light. It can be assumed that electromagnetic waves are actual light waves but only dealt with by different systems. Discovering the hidden third system has meant discovering acoustic waves when we think. This is what we measure to know the language of the brain.

The sounds produced when we think are of different noise decibels and frequencies.

The sounds produced by the brain when we think like I said can be measured but must be amplified to be able to be recorded and heard by modern equipment. The device is built according to the invention notes in the first book and will be able to record these sounds. These sounds can be heard at -45 decibels.

These sounds to be heard have frequencies between 21 Hz to 42 Hz with noise levels of -45db.

The sample rate is 44100 with stereo type.

The musical note for the sound of clapping recording when thinking about clapping is E10 [-231 Hz to 210 Hz]

Below diagram is the mp3 wave for the recorded thinking of clapping by the brain.

I had to amplify and change the graphs so that it can be seen on the screen.

Even though it is about 804 milliseconds long there are only two parts that respond to the system. The first two identical parts trigger the sequence of clapping as described above. The other bit down the line activates the vibrations that represent the escape or absorption of the waves to the body or ground.

This is the recorded command of the brain when someone thinks about clapping.

It sounds like the sound made when the tongue is out, and you are creating the crrrrrrrrr sound.

People, this is the sound of the brain when thinking about clapping.

Click here now to hear the sound.

https://img1.wsimg.com/blobby/go/e8972857-57d8-43db-80d4-9913437629c9/downloads/Clapping%20recording%20when%20thinking%20only%20david%20go.mp3?ver=1678828335216

This is how the sound looks on a wave pad graph. The only parts that make the body responds to the sound are the two identical parts just before the red line. These are the commands and the only ones that produce the crrrrrrr sound. Just at the end of the screen is another dhoti sound that gives the vibrations effects.

The whole purpose of starting with the sound made by clapping as I explained at the beginning is the fact that a lot of phone applications and some lights utilizes this clapping technology as a switch. Clap to switch on and off lights.

Now that we have a sound that means clapping, we can easily replace the clapping sound and make the system recognize the sound instead, but the issue is that when we think the sound decibels of thinking are -45 db. An amplifier must be incorporated to the system to be able to use thinking as an operating or command input.

But obviously you have seen the breakthrough.

Now what a person needs to do is simply think about clapping and with reverse engineering the system will identify the sequence and locate the switch to either switch off and on the device.

Just by thinking.

If we reverse the sequence and start from the bottom vibrations.

To the downward motion.

To the actual clapping.

To the elbow that received and forwarded or sent the commands.

To the right ear vibrations.

Then the right back side of the body.

The body itself will imitate clapping if everything is done correctly.

I have revolutionized the world we know today. Fitting for the first world global president.

This is just the beginning.

Now the world without any risks of operating in the brain and no need for any operation now this invention can be used inside gadgets like phones. This is step two of the invention. Instead of operating on the lumbar bone. Now the miniature rotary propeller that activates the electromagnetic waves can be made so small and included inside smart phones and devices to be able to use brain thoughts as an input command or even as an operating system.

This is my invention, and the patent is already in the first Volume I book dated 28 March 2022.

This is in the belief that an ISBN can establish the invention as a pre-booking for the patent to be registered with the official department.

I explained the basics of developing the brain thinking language so that we create a global stencil to be used by all.

But there are a lot of basic ground level things we must put in place to be able to do this on a global scale.

1. We need a dictionary of the brain's thinking process.
2. We need the vocabulary of the brain thinking process.
3. We need vowels of thinking, language construction rules and properties.
4. We need a brain word map to know exactly where words and what words are stored where.
5. Some of this information is freely available on the net from previous research.

6. Above all we need a dictionary and encyclopedia of brain thinking. This must include all the sounds made when we are thinking about anything.
7. We need to know where the brain stores, where and why.
8. We will need manufactures out there to test my invention in gadgets to make this brain decoding and thoughts as a global universal language as they pay me royalties etc. for the invention.

I can easily create all sounds produced when a person is thinking about anything. Like I said before; the brain, stores the words associated with a man in the right segment of the brain. And everything to do with woman on the left side. But sometimes other words can occupy different positions and other words can be found in more than one segment. But this is to do with association with the most use-case of that segment.

This is the interesting part.

First, I will devise and invent the brain language to describe common words and actions.

I follow the rules I have invented above that the language must consist of several factors up to six.

1. Use of the brain word location map of the brain.
2. Effects like vibrations and which side of the brain.
3. The place of the commands to trigger that action.
4. The actual body parts to perform that action.
5. The sounds and effects of the action.
6. The vibrations or results of the action and how they escape the system.

Having said that, lets do not waste time and jump straight into constructing our brain's thinking language.

One as a number.

1. Rights back side of the head.
2. Vibrations in the right ear.
3. Twinkling in the eyelid of the right ear.
4. Deflation of the body with shoulders slumping down.

One hundred.

1. Right back side of the brain.
2. Right ear mild vibrations.
3. Mild thump vibrations.
4. Deflation of the body down.

Two hundred.

1. Right back side of the brain.
2. Right ear mild vibrations.
3. The top part of the thumb.
4. The second part of the thumb.
5. Then deflates downward.

Three hundred.

1. Right back side.
2. Right ear mild vibrations.
3. Top part of thump.
4. Second part of the thump.
5. Third part of the thump.
6. Deflates downward.

Touch.

1. Right part of the brain.
2. Right ear.
3. Left ear.
4. Left hand.

5. Right hand.
6. Downward movement to ground.

Cry

1. Centre top of brain.
2. Top part of the forehead just below the hair line.
3. Downward line across face to bottom of chin.
4. Then face and shoulders pulled down.

Join hands.

1. Top center of brain.
2. Elbow left.
3. Elbow right.
4. Deflates down.

Lick

1. Top center of the brain.
2. Point of the lick [lips, hands, cheeks etc.]
3. Deflates waist middle.

Warning.

1. Top center of brain.
2. Slight pressure in the left ear.
3. Slight pressure in the right ear.
4. Deflates downward.

Whistle

1. Top center of the brain.
2. Pressure on top lip.
3. Pressure on bottom lip.
4. Deflates down.

Clap hands.

1. Right back side of brain.
2. Right ear mild vibrations.
3. Pressure points left elbow.
4. Pressure points right elbow.
5. Imitating joined hands clapping in progress.
6. Produced sound deflates downward as absorbed by ground.

Exhale.

1. Right back side of brain.
2. Slight pressure nostrils.
3. Deflates downwards on waist towards right side.

Inflate.

1. Right back side.
2. Slight pressure nostrils.
3. Deflates downwards on waist to left side.

Awake open eyes.

1. Right back side.
2. Left eye.
3. Right eye.
4. Deflates down to left side at waist level.

Sleep.

1. Right back side.
2. Left side.
3. To the right side.
4. Deflates to the left side.

Listen.

1. Right back side.

2. Right ear mild vibrations.
3. Heart or chest deep deflates.
4. Shoulders slumps down.

End.

1. Right back side.
2. Right ear vibrations.
3. Twist to the left side about 45 degrees.

I

1. Right back side.
2. Right ear vibrations.
3. Head or chest deflates down.

Sound.

1. Right back side.
2. Right ear faint mild vibrations.
3. Left ear vibrations.

The.

1. Right back side.
2. Right ear vibrations.
3. Twist to the right about 45 degrees.

Horn.

1. Right back side.
2. Right ear mild vibrations.
3. Lower left stomach grumbling.

Tell.

1. Right back side.
2. Right ear vibrations.
3. Left ear vibrations.

4. Lower lip.
5. Upper lip.
6. Drag top lip down.

Apologize.

1. Right back side.
2. Quick twist to side.
3. Right chest or heart deflations heavy down.

Sing.

1. Right back side.
2. Right ear.
3. Left ear.
4. Circulation of emotions from the heart and out.

Hi.

1. Right back side.
2. Left ear.
3. Right ear.
4. Chest or heart vibrations.
5. Chest or heart deflations.

Beep.

1. Right back side.
2. Right ear.
3. Left armpit vibrations.

Run.

1. Right back side.
2. Right ear vibrations.
3. To left leg.
4. Right leg.
5. All soft tapings under feet.

Deflate.

1. Right back side.
2. Right ear vibrations.
3. Left chest or heart deflates.

Inflate.

1. Right back side.
2. Left ear.
3. Shift or slide to the right waist then down.

At.

1. Right back side.
2. Right ear.
3. Left ear vibrations.

Or.

1. Right back side.
2. Right ear vibrations.

Do.

1. Right back side.
2. Right ear vibrations.
3. Left side rib.
4. Slide to left.

Man.

1. Right back side.
2. Right ear vibrations.
3. Vibrations in the middle of the body just below the chest line.

Woman.

1. Left back side.
2. Left ear vibrations.
3. Right left part below chest vibrations and deflates.

Breath out.

1. Right back side.
2. Right ear vibrations.
3. Deflates but out stomach.

Breath in.

1. Right back side.
2. Right ear vibrations.
3. Inflates in the stomach.

Command.

1. Right back side.
2. Right ear vibrations.
3. Move or slide to the left.

Sit.

1. Right back side.
2. Right ear vibrations.
3. Slide to the left side at the waist.
4. Slide hard to right side at the waist.

Believe.

1. Right back side.
2. Right ear vibrations.
3. Heart deflates down.
4. Shift to the right.
5. Slide to the left.
6. Center.

President.

1. Right back side.
2. Right ear vibrations.
3. Chest deflates.
4. Shift to left at waist.
5. Shift to right at waist.
6. Pat back vibrations on backbone.
7. Deflates down.

I.

1. Right back side.

2. Right ear vibrations.

3. Bend back outward at waist.

Am.

1. Right back side.
2. Right ear vibrations.
3. Deflates down fast.

Start.

1. Right back side.
2. Right Shoulder deflates down.

Stop.

1. Right back side.
2. Right shoulder.
3. Slide to the left waist point.

Pause.

1. Right back side.
2. Vibrations under the left side chest.

Break.

1. Right back side.
2. Middle part below chest line vibrations and hand vibrations.

Accelerate.

1. Right back side.
2. Right chest side vibrations and deflations down fast.

Reduce speed.

1. Right back side.
2. Right chest deflates.

Turn left.

1. Right back side.
2. Rotate right to left in 45 degrees.

Turn right.

1. Right back side.
2. Rotate left to right at 45 degrees.

Look left.

1. Right back side.
2. Left side eye mild vibrations.
3. Left side head vibrations.

Paper.

1. Right back side.
2. Right top side. Mild head vibrations.
3. Twisting to the left then.
4. Twisting to the right and back center.

Plastic.

1. Right back side.
2. Left top side.
3. Mild head vibrations.
4. Twisting to right then to left.
5. Back at center.

Bicycle.

1. Right back side.
2. Top head vibrations.
3. Twist to the left eight times.
4. Then one complete revolution.
5. Deflates and centers.

Ask.

1. Right back side.
2. Right ear vibrations.
3. Left ear.
4. Slide at waistline to the right then left.

Beg.

1. Right back side.
2. Right ear vibrations.
3. Left ear vibrations.
4. Left then bend backwards.

Come.

1. Right back side.
2. Right ear vibrations.
3. Left ear.
4. Bent backwards.

Go.

1. Right back side.
2. Right ear vibrations. Bent forward.

Accept.

1. Right back side.
2. Right ear vibrations.
3. Left chest vibrations.
4. Slide outwards to the left.

Like.

1. Right back side.
2. Right ear vibrations.
3. Great shift to left at waist from right.

Shake.

1. Right back side.
2. Right ear vibrations.
3. Move hip to right at waist.
4. Move hip to left at waist level.
5. Then slide hard to the right at waist.

Drive.

1. Right back side.
2. Right ear vibrations.
3. Chest vibrations.
4. Slide hard to the right side.

Switch.

1. Right back side.
2. Chest deflates fast.

Remote.

1. Right back side.
2. Left chest.
3. Fast deflates to the left.

Change.

1. Right back side.
2. Left chest mild vibrations.
3. Rotate 45 degrees left to right.

Channel.

1. Right back side.
2. Mild anus vibrations. [Do not laugh]

Radio.

1. Right back side.
2. Right ear vibrations.
3. Chest deflates fast.

Television.

1. Right er vibrations.
2. Slight head twist.

Play.

1. Right back side.
2. Right ear vibrations.
3. Left chest vibrations.
4. Deflates out to left.

Power on.

1. Right back side.
2. Right ear vibrations.
3. Left ear.

4. Right chest vibrations.
5. Left chest vibrations.

Power off.

1. Right back side.
2. Left ear vibrations.
3. Chest vibrations.
4. Deflates move to the right.

Open.

1. Right back side.
2. Right ear vibrations.
3. Right ear.
4. Left ear.
5. Move swiftly or slide to the left outside.

Close.

1. Right back side.
2. Right ear vibrations.
3. Move or slide to the right at the waistline.

Donate.

1. Right back side.
2. Right ear vibrations.
3. Left elbow vibrations
4. Right elbow vibration.
5. Slide backward at waistline.
6. Swirl in the stomach.

Follow.

1. Right back side.
2. Right ear vibrations.
3. Slide at waistline to left.

I kiss you.

1. Right back side.
2. Right chest side pressure.
3. Left side chest pressure.

Interpret.

1. Right back side.
2. Right chest pressure.
3. Left chest then deflates.

Talk.

1. Right back side.
2. Right ear vibrations.
3. Left ear vibrations.
4. Chest left side deflates.

Smiles.

1. Right back side.
2. Actual pulling of muscle to imitate smiling.

I like you.

1. Right back side.
2. Right side pressure.
3. Left side deflates heavily.

I see you.

1. Right back side.
2. Left eye.
3. Right eye.
4. Deflates at waistline more like bending down at stomach level.

I fancy you.

1. Right back side.
2. Fast right knee inwards bend to the other.

I adore you.

1. Right back side.
2. Bend your knee right in front fast.

Shout.

1. Right back side.
2. Upside jaw and vibrates.

Hands.

1. Right back side.
2. Actual pointing at the hands.

Speak.

1. Right back side.
2. Middle of the body below the chest line.
3. Pressure on top lip.
4. Pressure on bottom lip.

Slippers.

1. Right back side.
2. Actual left and right slippers.

Please.

1. Right back side.
2. Chest heart side pressure and deflates.

Peace.

1. Right back side.
2. Chest heart side pressure and bent knees.

Kick.

1. Right back side.
2. Actual kicks and bent knees.

Run.

1. Right back side.
2. Dot fast right leg.

I love you.

1. Right back side.
2. Left chest pressure.
3. Right chest pressure.

Swallow.

1. Right back side.
2. Actual imitates of swallowing and deflating down. Bending at waistline.

Think.

1. Right back side.
2. Side right head pressure and deflating down.

Horny.

Tickling of private parts.

Yawn.

1. Right back side.
2. Close eyes and slump down.

Yawn can also be one. Right back side.

Deflates.

Pressure in the middle of the body below the chest line.

Squats.

1. Right back side.
2. Actual squatting with bent knees.

Fart.

1. Right back side.
2. Actual whirlwind in the stomach and exhaust deflates.

Fingers.

1. Right back side.
2. Actual pressure-counting of all fingers from the left hand starting with the thumb. Counts all then moves to the right hand.

Ribs.

1. Right back side.
2. Actual ribs left then right.

Blood.

1. Right back side.
2. Then all over the body where there is blood.

Spine.

1. Left side of the brain.
2. Then actual pressure on all spines.

Hair.

1. Center to the left back of the brain.

2. Pressure vibrations on all hair.

Testicles.

1. Right back side.
2. Right chest.
3. Center bottom below chest line.
4. Left chest.
5. Both testicles.

Breath.

1. Right back side.
2. Path the air flows; nose, lungs and out of nostrils.

Mucus.

1. Right back side.
2. Spine back and the nose.

Sperm.

1. Right back side.
2. Right testicle.
3. Left testicle.
4. Circles in the head of the penis and deflates.

Feces.

1. Right back side.
2. Describes food path until out.
3. Deflates.

See.

1. Right back side.
2. Describes in the flow of seeing circulating in eyes then deflates.

Deflates.

1. Right back side.
2. Actual deflates.

Pee.

1. Right back side.
2. Actual emotion of peeing.

Kill.

Actual twist of the head and neck.

Sugar.

1. Right back side.
2. Salivating.

Salt.

1. Right back side.
2. Emotion of bitter.

Drunk.

1. Right back side.
2. Eyes closes and slumps as if asleep.

Sleep.

1. Right back side.
2. Sleep feeling and slumping.

Legs.

1. There are no points in the brain where legs are stored as a word. [But to be clarified]
2. Legs as a word is stored in the legs.

Same as hands, naval, toes, buttocks, and stomach.

Nose.

1. Right back side.
2. Actual nose plus deflating backward.

Mouth, lips, ears, cheeks, eyebrows, iris all stored in the right back side and points to actual parts of the body.

Forehead points to the right back side and the actual forehead then deflates.

Tongue.

1. Right the back side.
2. The actual tongue.
3. The direction deep down throat where it extends.

Heartbeat.

1. Right back side.
2. Actual vibrations in the heart.
3. Deflates down.

Liver.

1. Right back side.
2. Liver.
3. Deflating down.

Kidney.

1. Right back side.
2. Left chest.
3. Middle of the body below the chest line.

4. Plus, actual organ.

Lung.

1. Right back side.
2. Right side below chest.
3. Then the actual organ.

Heart.

1. Right back side.
2. Right side below chest.
3. Left side below chest.
4. Then the heart itself.

Eyes.

1. Right eye.
2. Left eye.
3. Right place below the chest.
4. Left place below the chest.
5. Deflates down.

Test.

1. Right back side.
2. Left ear vibrations.
3. Right ear vibrations
4. Slide to the left fast.

Slow down.

1. Right back side.
2. Deflates heavy back to left.

Close the window.

1. Right back side.
2. Right ear.

3. Deflates shoulder down.

Father.

1. Right back side.
2. Left side below chest.
3. Right chest
4. Deep deflates.

Mother.

1. Left back side.
2. Right below the chest.
3. Deflates down.

Rotate.

1. Right back side.
2. Right to left rotates.

Open door.

1. Right back door.
2. Soft anus open. [Try not to laugh.]
3. Chest heart side deflates down.

Close door.

1. Right back side.
2. Anus close.
3. Chest heart side deflates.

Together.

1. Right back side.
2. Right cheek vibrations.
3. Left cheek vibrations.
4. Right chest vibrations.
5. Deflation.

Real.

1. Right back side.
2. Right eye.
3. Left eye.
4. Left chest deflates.

Write.

1. Right back side.
2. Right eye.
3. Left eye.
4. Index finger vibrations.
5. Left chest deflations.

Left.

1. Right back side.
2. Right eye.
3. Left eye.
4. Right chest vibrations.
5. Slide at waist level to right then to left.

Left eye.

1. Right back side.
2. Right eye vibrations.
3. Left eye vibrations.
4. Slide to the right at waist level.
5. Slide to the left at waist level.

Fast.

1. Lower back neck vibrations. Drop down shoulders as deflating fast.

Forward.

1. Right back side.
2. Right hand elbow clicks and vibration. Bending down backward leaning forward.

Next.

1. Right back side.
2. Right back elbow tap.
3. Bend forward.

When.

1. Right back side.
2. Left ear vibrations.
3. Bend on the waist to the left side.

Why?

1. Right back side.
2. Side head shake.
3. Bend forward at waist level.

Who?

1. Right back side.
2. Left ear vibrates.
3. Bend forward but to the left side at waist level.

Was.

1. Right back waist.
2. Slight left ear shake.
3. Bend to left at waist fast.

Park.

1. Right back side.
2. Right ear vibrations.
3. Deflates bending down.

Reverse.

1. Right back side.
2. Click right ear.
3. Deflates bending down.

U-turn.

1. Right back side.
2. Right ear vibrations.
3. Anticlockwise turn.

Horn.

1. Right back side.
2. Right ear vibrations.
3. Left ear vibrations.

Shut down.

1. Right bottom neck soft vibrations.
2. Left stomach deflates.

Enter.

1. Right back side.
2. Right hand muscle clicks.

Click.

1. Right back side.
2. Back right head soft click.

Computer.

1. Right back side.
2. Neck tightening.
3. Back shoulders deflate and drop.
4. Bending down.

In this chapter I will list all words and functions that fall in each category. This is the easiest way to know the commands. Like I said at the beginning the brain is divided into four major categories.

7. The right front part.
8. The left front part.
9. The right back part of the brain.
10. The left back part of the brain.

Some words seemed to have been repeated. This is because in the brain they appear at different locations or have slight different commands. I tried these from several positions that sometimes I got different results. I have discovered that thinking a word while sleeping, or standing or even sleeping or dreaming will result in different construction patterns.

Do not frate. We will understand all this with time. Some definitions might work for you than for others.

I will list all the functions that fall in the right back part first. [More in volume IV.] As everything to do with commands and actions is likely to fall into this category. But like I also said some functions and words can also be found in other segments of the brain.

The Right back part of the Brain.

Yours, am, how, thinking, I, he, brain, cuddle, is, science, love, what, kiss, does, does, all numbers, peace, Jesus, God, Holy spirit, man, beer, research, sex, alcohol, brush, green, make-love, January to December, Wednesday, Thursday, head, stomach are, thigh, sausage, hair, zebra, all country names, Sunday, lion, planets, Friday, Saturday, good.

Socks, shoes, trousers, plus, vegetables, labels, and print.

The left back side of the brain.

Tuesday, you, Monday, mother, sweet, war, evil, beautiful, she, woman, names.

The right front side of the brain.

Apple, polish, football, pineapple, decoding.

Right at the center front of the brain.

Apple, salad, coffee, sugar, tea, chocolate.

The center of the back brain.

Dress, pants, bra.

Now let us look at the recordings of the sounds that make the invention a reality with so many possibilities.

The best things are that you do not need an expensive MRI etc. You get a rotary propeller from a miniature drone and adjust it to be attached to the device and to the person in a perpendicular angle to the brain.

This is because of James Maxwell's discovery that electromagnetic waves travel at the same speed as light. The waves travel perpendicular to each other from the source. So it does not mean that the device can be in the brain. The device can be at waist level as long as it is perpendicular to the emitted waves.

I argued also that there is a secret third system in the human body. That uses light waves and turn these to acoustic waves. These are the waves we will try to record. But these waves cannot be heard by our naked ears. So a person is asked to think whilst wearing the rotary propeller that produces and amplifies the electromagnetic waves. When we speak, we produce sound waves. But what about when we simply think.

Yes, we produce electromagnetic waves. Which are not destroyed or converted by the body. But these are absorbed and resent by the system. This is the critical point. So, nothing is lost. These waves are simply absorbed by the body or surfaces. That process of absorption produces vibrations we can measure as well.

So, a dreaming person or a thinking person can still produce the third inner system's language as MP3 sound, but they are magnetic-light waves converted to acoustic.

These when amplified sounds like what happens with your tongue when saying the crrrrr sound with your tongue vibrating.

This is the language of the brain that is critical in understanding brain thoughts.

Welcome to Tomorrow's World Order.

Initially it is difficult to hear the sounds emitted.

A person is asked to think of a thought. This is recorded as the first step.

The second part is to think about the same thought but while mouth is shut. Then loudly think the thought while not emitting words. So, the first is silent thinking. The second is thinking while actually saying the words silently without sound.

The two recordings are recorded by a simple voice recorder.

Download NCH Mix pad multitrack software.

https://www.nch.com.au/mixpad/index.html?ns=true&kw=mixpad%20sound%20editor&gclid=Cj0KCQjwtsCgBhDEARIsAE7RYh28LbA7-uj7imaEgcFTSX7Qt2de6PflwrPxYx5w2cFvarAkbE9Xh7AaAvnaEALw_wcB

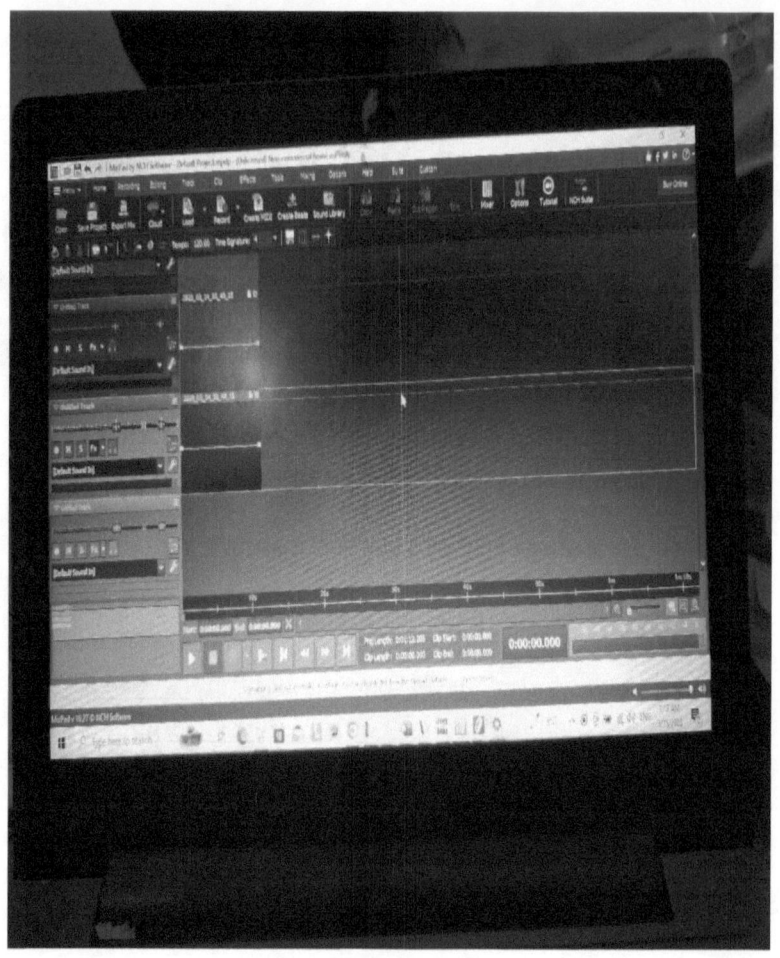

Open the Mix Pad.

Open the mp3 file from your device you have recorded using any voice recorder app.

Then upload at least five of the same mp3. Do not worry if you cannot hear anything at first when you play the mp3.

You have some adjustments to do first to be audible.

Once you have uploaded all five of the same mp3 in each layer on the mix pad.

Now it is time to adjust the tracks.

You must amplify all the tracks one by one.

Click on FX on each Untitled Track. [Of each track you have uploaded.]

This brings an option screen.

Choose Volume. Click.

Then click Amplify.

Then increase the gain percentage to four hundred.

Repeat this for all tracks at least five of the same recording. Do one recording at a time. The five are duplicates of the same and not the other version where a person thinks out loud. It is just one track of just the normal thinking x 5 of them.

Once that is done for all tracks. That means you have easily amplified the track to human audible levels.

Just set it to 400 percent gain and close the page. Click the X. Back to the mix pad.

But first write down the path where the project will be saved. It shows the path where it says Output File.

Write this down normally its in your documents/ mix pad Projects/Default project.mp3

Now click on Export Mix.

Now click Export.

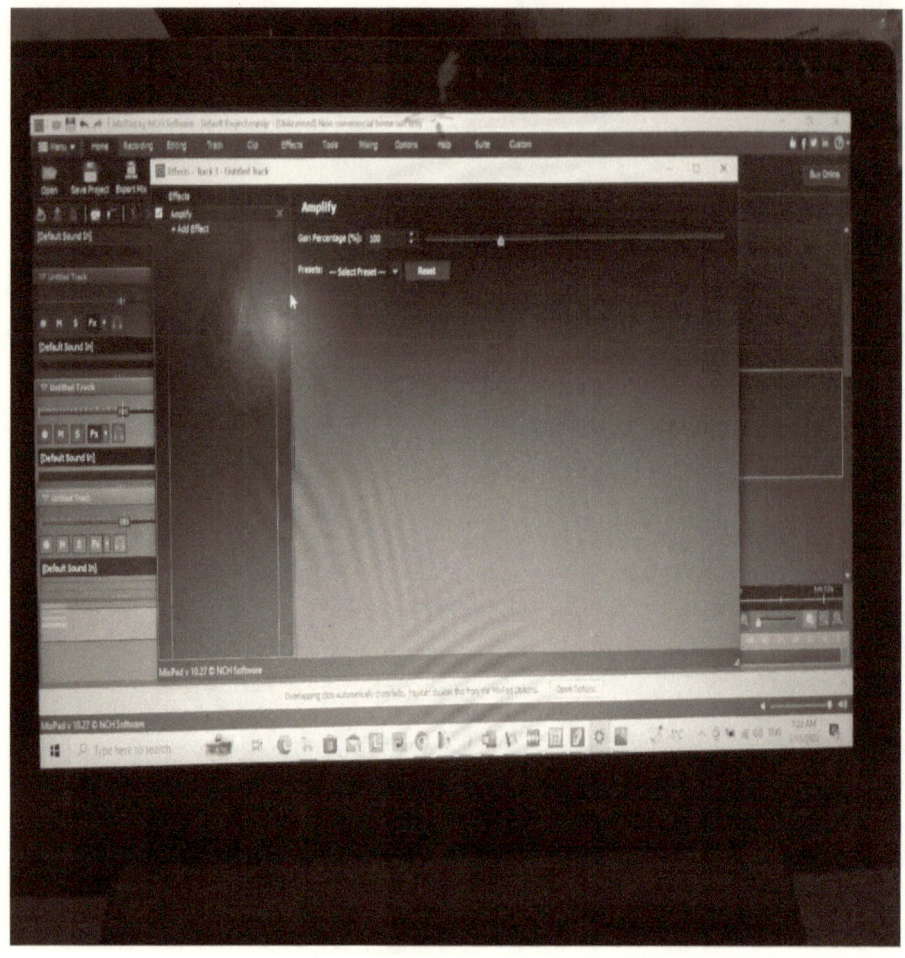

Wait for the project to be exported.

Now go to the project file to retrieve our amplified track.

It is a good idea to make a copy and rename the copy only. Leave the Default project track but keep it in a different project folder than this as any new project will erase this one.

Rename the track so that you will be able to identify it. Secondly if you make mistakes you still have the original to work with.

Now you need a different sound wave pad.

You need a Wavepad. Click this link.

https://www.nch.com.au/wavepad/index.html?ns=true&kw=nch%
20wavepad&gclid=Cj0KCQjwtsCgBhDEARIsAE7RYh1MbRCfR
grGiZxtnRFpAw6ajyQKVIiI6wRpK2ipP8-
6fdkOsPqJgZYaApHgEALw_wcB

Installing this takes a few minutes and the first two to three uses
are free so try not to make mistakes. Unless you can pay for the
software if you want to use it for several attempts.

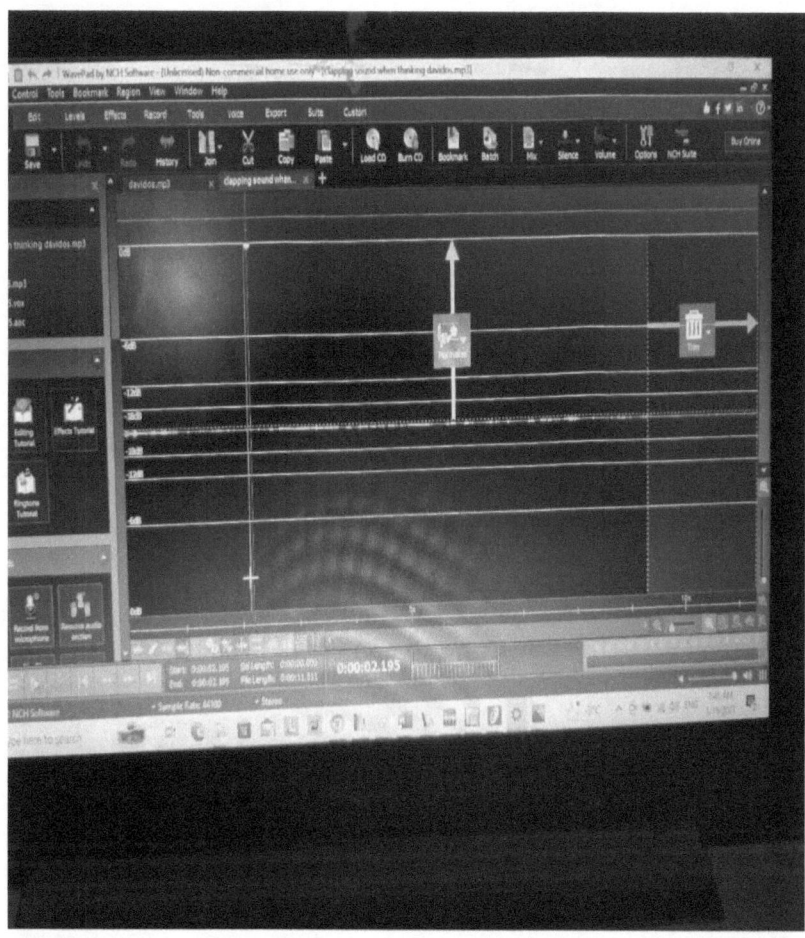

This is how this will look before any adjustments. Now if everything went well you will be able to hear the crrrrr noises from the sound if you click on play button.

First click in the left-hand corner.

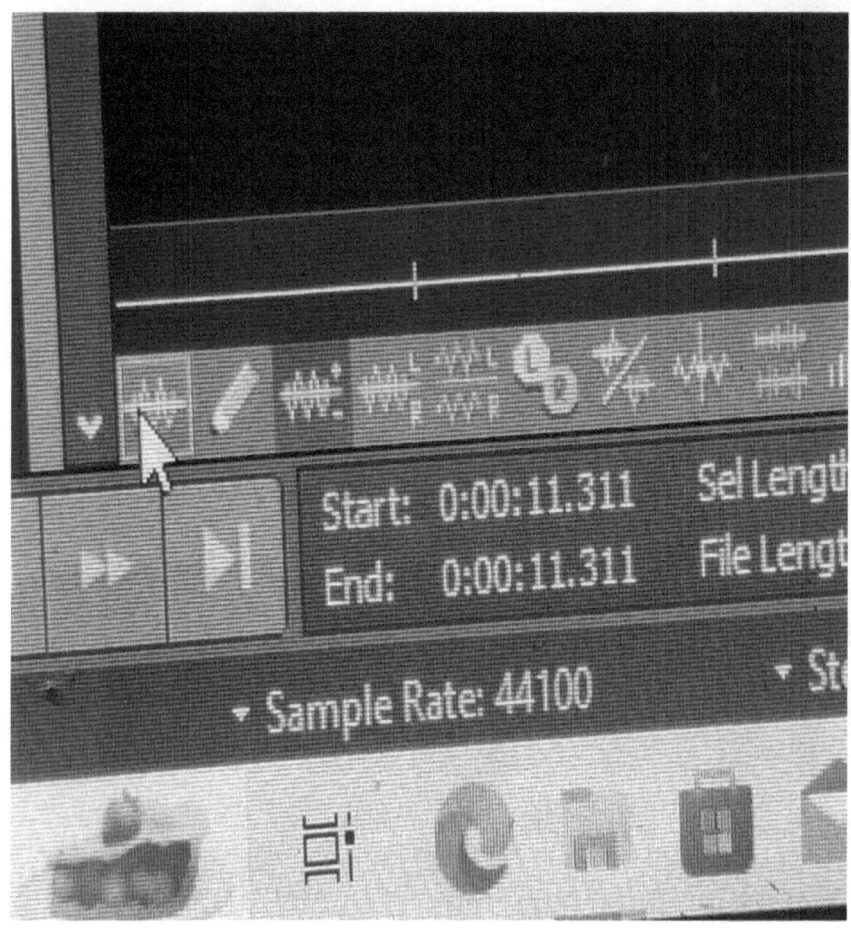

Once done then click in the right-hand corner a little bit up where there is a plus sign to increase the wavelength. See diagram below.

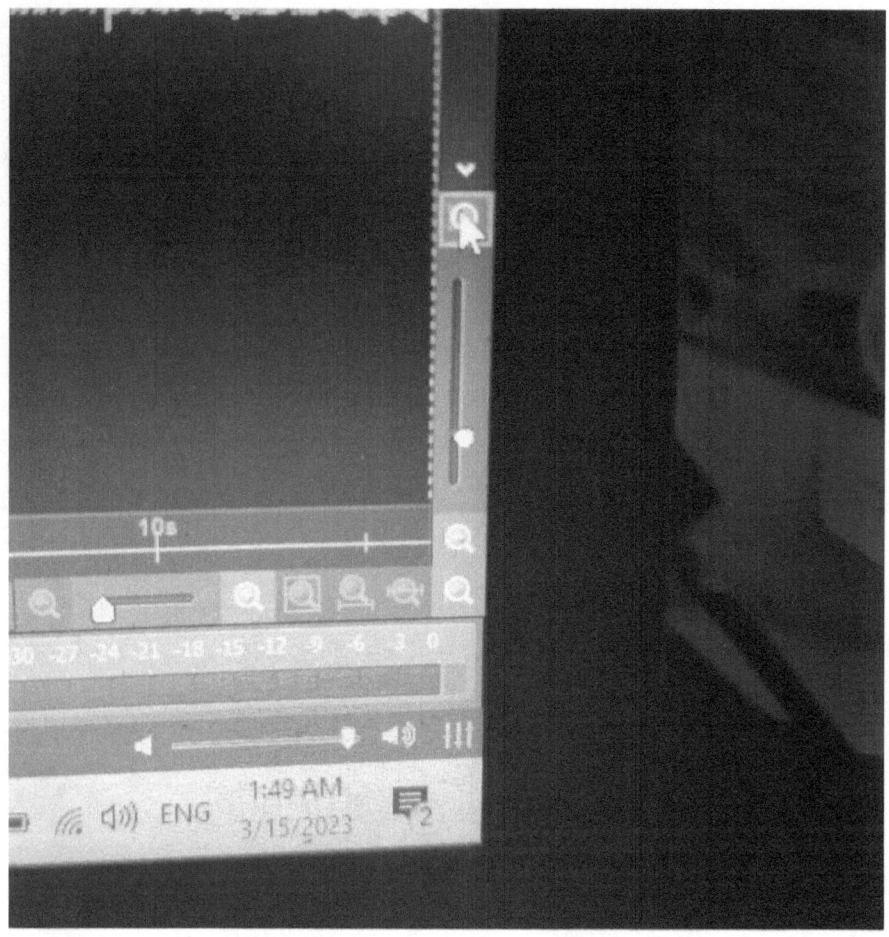

After expanding the wave size.

Now we need to include the frequency spectrogram with algorithmic scale. Click the third button from right. See diagram below.

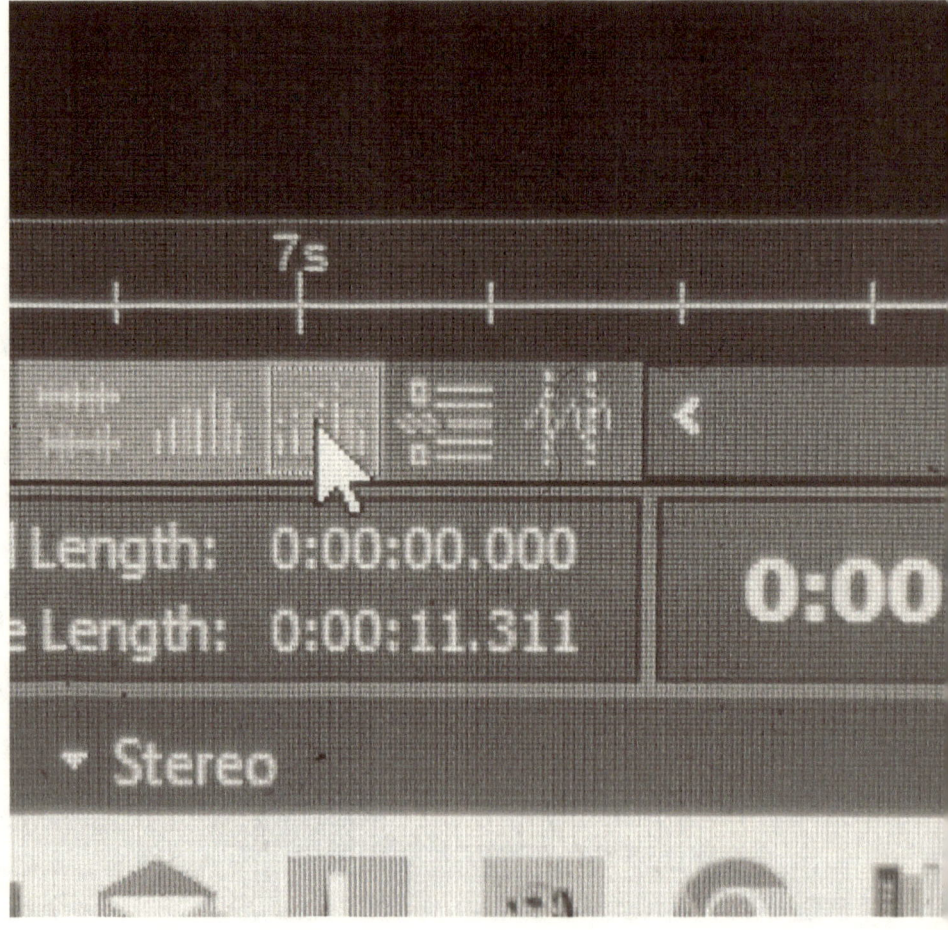

Once that is done the Wavepad will look like the one below.

 Now you can see the waves.

You can see the pattern.

Now click play and listen to funny sounds especially the crrrrr. If you can hear this congratulations, you have recorded brain thoughts. But you must understand that without the invented rotary devices I mentioned in the first book this might be impossible. This device converts and emits the electromagnetic waves and acoustic waves to be able to decode these.

Do not expect miracles do it right.

Usually, it is only a few patterns that have an effect on the system as these contain the actual recorded thoughts. But it all depends on what the thought was about. At first just an innovative idea to start with just one action like we did. Just with clapping. Then for sure decode this and replay. You will find out that the device does reverse engineering in that it tells you what the sequence you just played means.

It is like talking to the third inner system. Asking it a question.

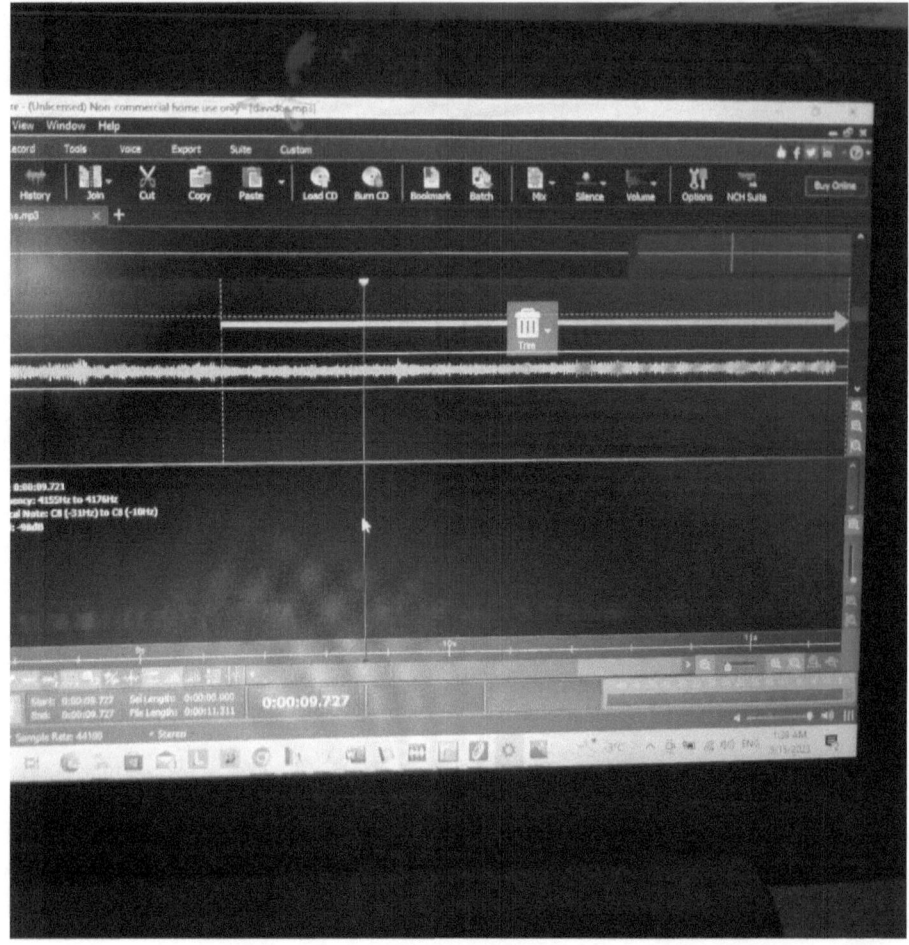

Where if you mention the sequence of clapping in reverse order. The system tells you that its clapping as it actually imitates the clapping. You might feel like the hands are put together and you are clapping.

But the trick is that the system when it uses a magnetic propeller makes the system act like a human brain. Recording and storing actions and activities. When you play the recording, the system goes back to search where it has stored the clapping activity the first time it heard this and replays that clapping.

This is the trick because we are doing exactly like what the brain does in real life. So, electromagnetism makes this system do it artificially.

So now if the subjects think about clapping. The system points to the right side of the brain. Then the left elbow. The right elbow. Hands together. Downward movements of the sound to the ground and the escape therefore deflation.

If you play the recording. The system repeats the process as if you are telling it to clap. This is the tricky as we are going to use this aspect to replace the sound noise that activates switches with this crrrrrr sound. So that whatever system we make will only need to hear the crrrrr noises to activate. Now including amplifier and heavy microphones the person only needs to think about clapping.

The device records or inputs the sound to activate the switch.

The frequency spectrogram with algorithmic scale gives a lot of information we can use to manually construct the sounds using music. It tells you the musical notes E10, A4 etc.

I also believe that this graph will match the fMRI graph that can be recorded from brain activity. So, you can tell which part has an effect on the brain. In the example only three parts make the system react. So, the rest could simply be noises.

Another thing is that you must record in a noise tight environment for better results.

Now if blown up the Wavepad should look something like this. Now you are able to see clearly which waves make the system react.

You can choose to reduce the noise levels. I have discovered that at -45 dB the wave and sounds are crystal clear but might not be best for you. Try what works for you.

But if you check at the bottom right corner at the noise decibel part. You will discover that the wave pattern that reacts to the system is at -45 db.

I think this might decide success or failure. Until we are 100 percent sure. I think try to adjust to -45 db. At one point it just happened automatically.

Wavepad has a lot of effects which you can use to improve the quality, but it is not necessary. Take note of the frequency in Hertz etc. Then save the mp3.

Then from now on you have an activating key that replaces the sound of clapping. Now you can use this sound as the check key. Every time a person thinks the microphones will record this sound to match the check sum key to activate the system.

You can do all this fast and cost free. After all, the system uses drone technology as well for the manipulation of electromagnetic waves.

You must read the first books where I explained the techniques to be used to improve the accuracy. You must know the delayed time-space continuum mechanism.

GitHub has several projects using the clap mechanism. Now we can easily replace the clap sound with this new sound of how the brain interprets clapping to use as the activating switch.

This is my version of clapping as interpreted by the brain.

Click here. Or copy and paste.

https://img1.wsimg.com/blobby/go/e8972857-57d8-43db-80d4-9913437629c9/downloads/Clapping%20recording%20when%20thinking%20only%20david%20go.mp3?ver=1678828335216

If everyone in the world follows what is in this book it follows too that the sound of clapping will be the same. That makes apps that use brain language, thought, and dreams universal. Imagine the possibilities.

I will make several sounds made by every word in the English dictionary. But all this will be in Volume IV of the book. There are so many possibilities that I can write up to twenty volumes on this topic alone. Imagine using the same invention to make people with damaged body parts be able to do what they couldn't do.

I promised I will decode the language of the brain, thoughts and dreams and I just did.

The future has just begun.

Datestamp / Timestamp 28 MARCH 2022.

David Gomadza

[15 March 2023]

The First Global President of the world.

Tomorrow's World Order

www.twofuture.world

info@twofuture.world

00447719210295

Everything we are publishing for now is free but if this works for you then you are obliged to donate. Simply visit our website www.twofuture.world and donate.

Do you want to know the sound made by the brain when a person thinks about donating?

First let us construct the language pattern.

Donate.

1. Right back side.
2. Right ear vibrations.
3. Left elbow vibrations
4. Rights elbow vibration.
5. Slide backward at waistline.
6. Swirl in the stomach.

This is the language of the brain.

Listen to this.

Donate. Copy and paste or click.

https://img1.wsimg.com/blobby/go/e8972857-57d8-43db-80d4-9913437629c9/downloads/Donate.mp3?ver=1678849211168

Further reading.

The Greatshift. 2023 is the year of the GreatShift to sustainable energies.

Welcome to Tomorrow's World Order.

https://play.google.com/store/books/details/David_Gomadza_THE_GREATSHIFT?id=KH2xEAAAQBAJ&hl=en&gl=US

Signed

David Gomadza

First Global President

Dated 15 March 2023.

Volume IV to be published soon.

www.ingramcontent.com/pod-product-compliance
Lightning Source LLC
Chambersburg PA
CBHW030727180526
45157CB00008BA/3075